1000 SIGHT WORDS THE ULTIMATE VOCABULARY BOOK

PICTURE DICTIONARY WITH SENTENCE

English - Korean

action

행위

Action!

actually

사실은

I actually like strawberry.

adjective

형용사

Tell me an adjective to describe this.

afraid

두려워

What are you afraid of?

agreed

동의

They agreed on music.

ahead

앞으로

Who was ahead in the race?

allow

허용하다

Did the teacher allow him to go play?

apple

사과

Eat an apple.

arrived

도착

My plane arrived on time.

born

태어난

Where were you born?

bought

샀다

She bought new clothes.

British

영국인

Who is the British monarch?

capital

자본

The capital is in Washington DC.

chance

기회

Dice is a game of chance.

chart

차트

What does your medical chart say?

church

교회에

Did you go to church?

column

기둥

Did you read the newspaper column?

company

회사

What company do you work for?

conditions

정황

What are the weather conditions.

corn

옥수수

Do you like corn?

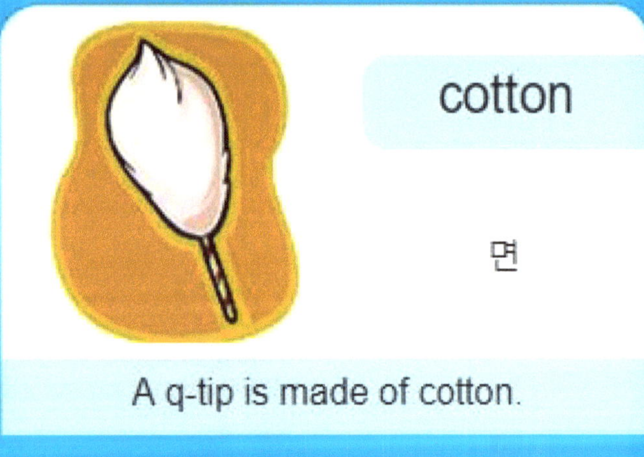

cotton

면

A q-tip is made of cotton.

cows

소

How many cows does he have?

create

창조하다

What art did you create?

dead

죽은

The bug is dead.

deal

거래

Did you agree on the deal?

death

죽음

The grim reaper is death.

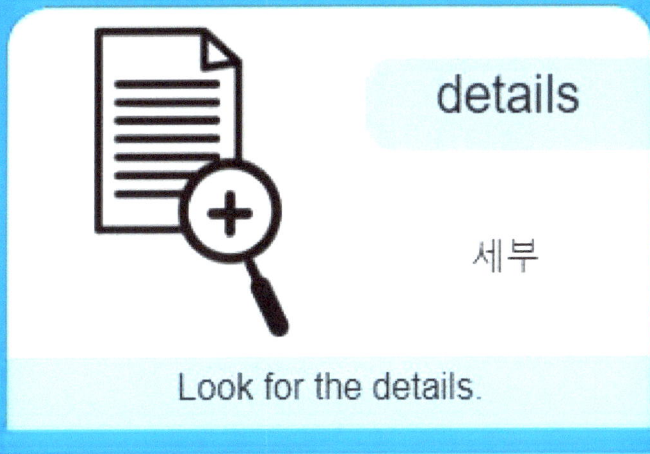

details

세부

Look for the details.

determine

결정

Did you determine where to go eat?

difficult

어려운

I found this difficult.

division

분할

We did division today.

doesn't

아니

Doesn't it sound beautiful?

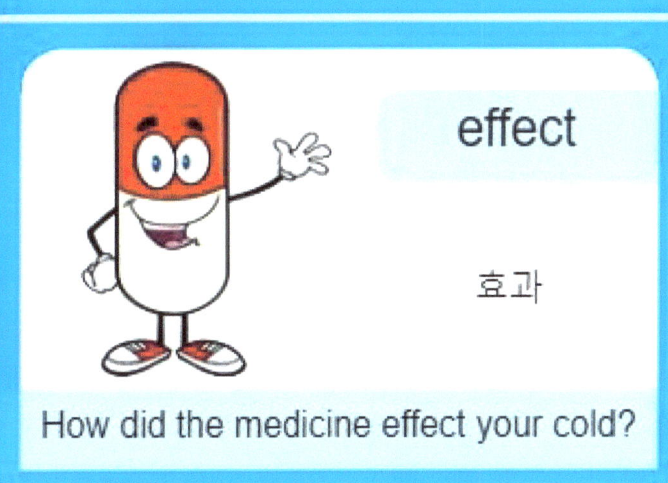

effect

효과

How did the medicine effect your cold?

entire

완전한

The entire family was in the picture.

especially

특별한

She especially liked writing.

evening

저녁

The ceremony was this evening.

experience

경험

She has a lot of experience.

factories

공장

There are a lot of factories there.

fair

재미있는 공원

Let's go to the fair.

fear

무서움

I have a huge fear of clowns.

fig

무화과

I ate a fig.

forward

앞으로

Spring forward the clocks.

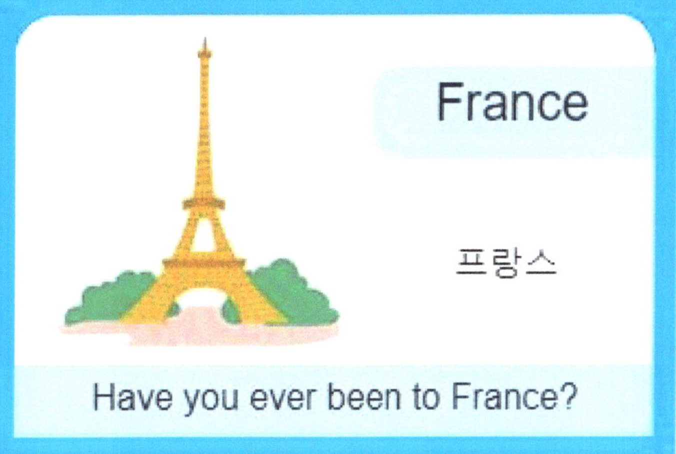

France

프랑스

Have you ever been to France?

fresh

신선한

All the fruit is fresh.

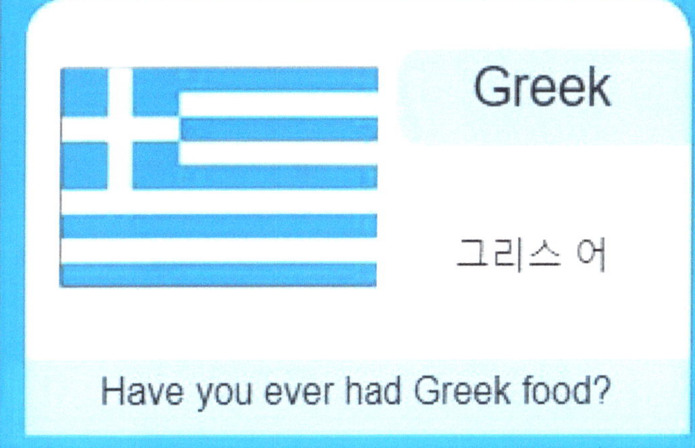

Greek

그리스 어

Have you ever had Greek food?

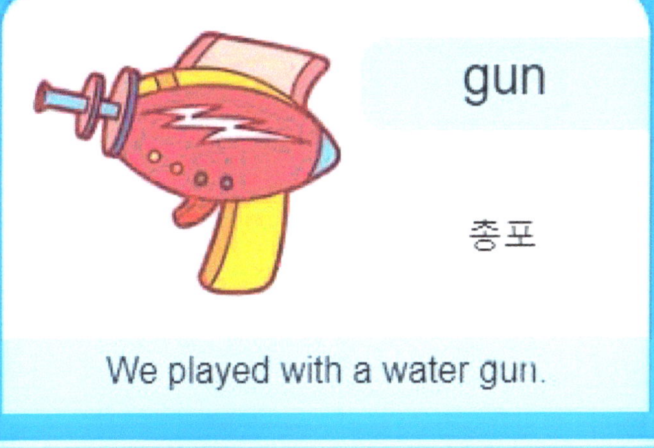

gun

총포

We played with a water gun.

hoe

괭이

Use a hoe in the garden.

huge

거대한

Those trees are huge!

isn't

그렇지 않다

Isn't it nice to hang out with friends?

led

리더

The dog led her.

level

수평

Use the level to hang the picture.

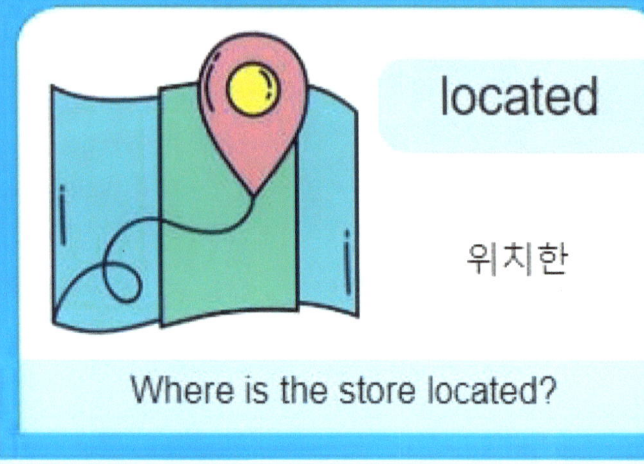

located

위치한

Where is the store located?

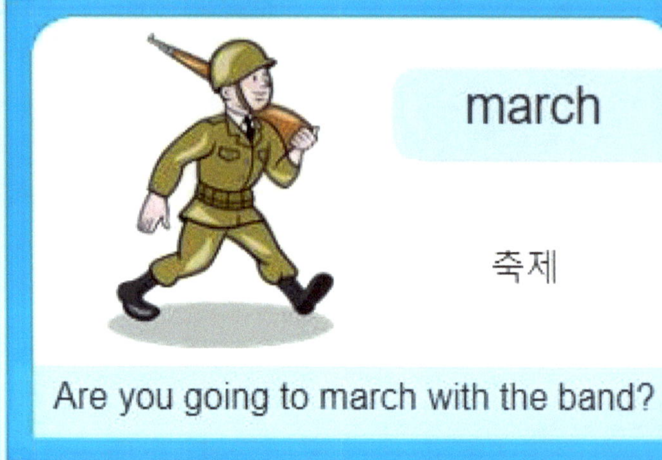

march

축제

Are you going to march with the band?

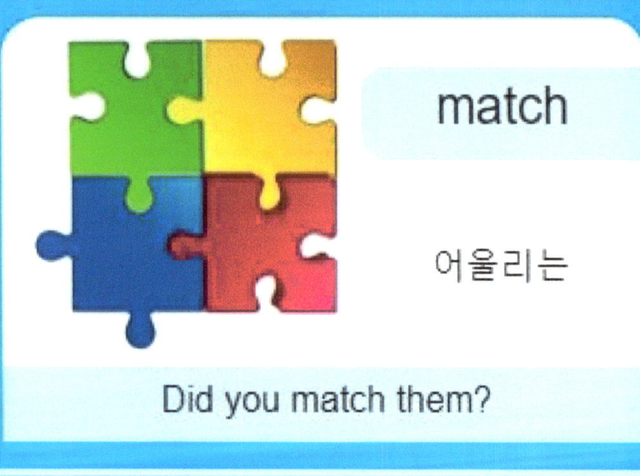

match

어울리는

Did you match them?

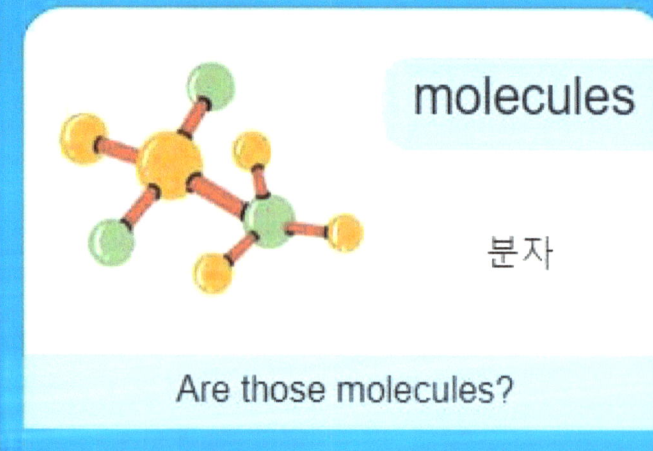

molecules

분자

Are those molecules?

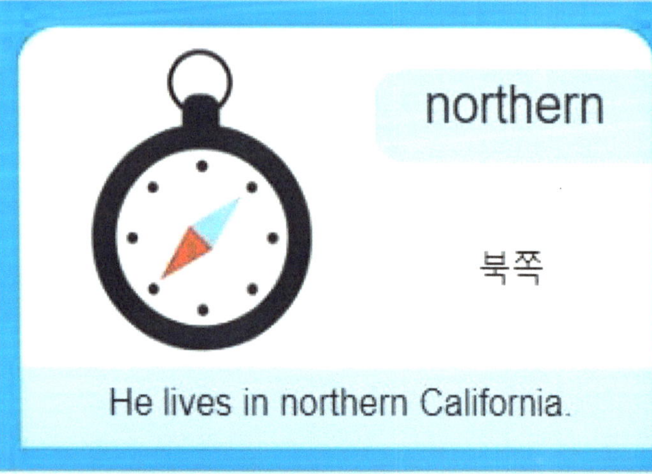

northern

북쪽

He lives in northern California.

nose

코

My nose is running.

office

사무실

Do you need any office supplies?

oxygen

산소

What is the symbol for oxygen?

plural

복수형

What is the plural of a mouse?

prepared

준비하다

She prepared for the exam.

pretty

예쁜

Pretty in pink.

printed

인쇄

She printed out the forms.

radio

라디오

Let's listen to the radio.

repeated

반복

They repeated the exercises daily.

rope

로프

Do you have any rope?

rose

장미

Thank you for the rose.

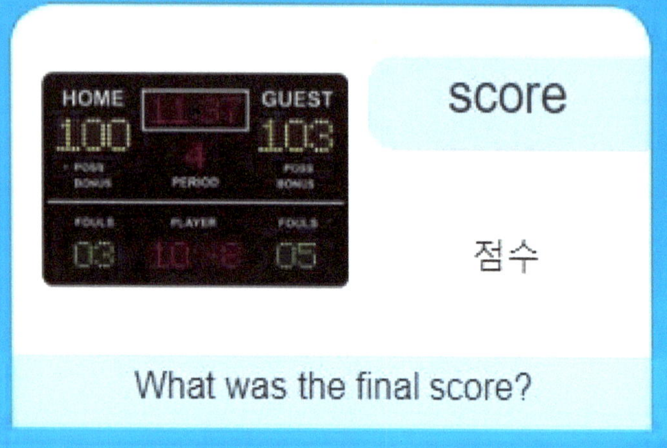

score

점수

What was the final score?

seat

좌석

The girls took a seat in the sand.

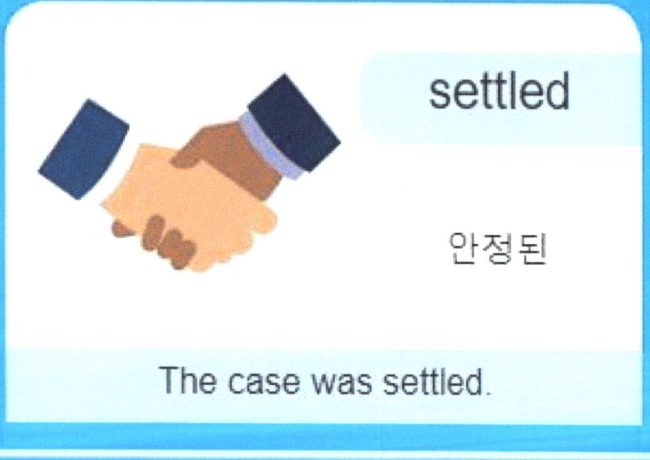

settled

안정된

The case was settled.

shoes

신발

Put your shoes on.

shop

상점

I'm need to go shop for groceries.

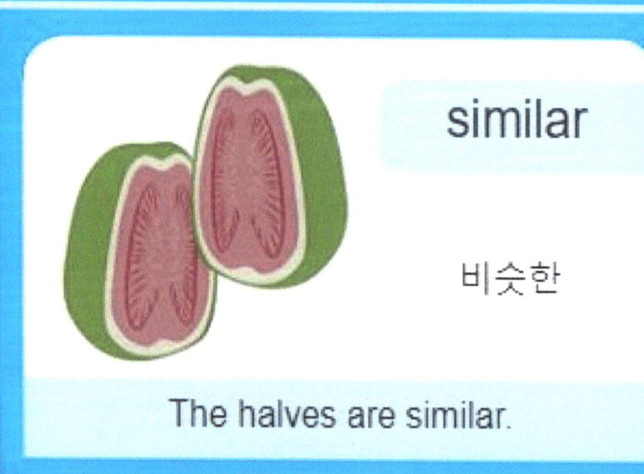

similar

비슷한

The halves are similar.

sir

경

Yes, sir!

sister

여자 형제

Is she your sister?

smell

냄새

I love the smell of cookies!

solution

해결책

I figured out a solution!

southern

남쪽

She's a southern belle.

steel

강철

The new building used steel.

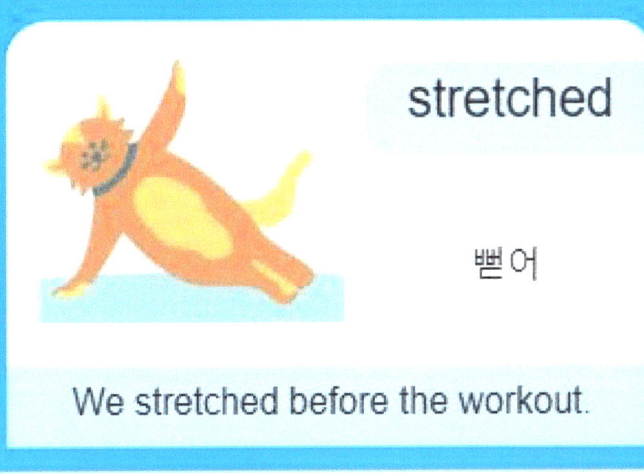

stretched

뻗어

We stretched before the workout.

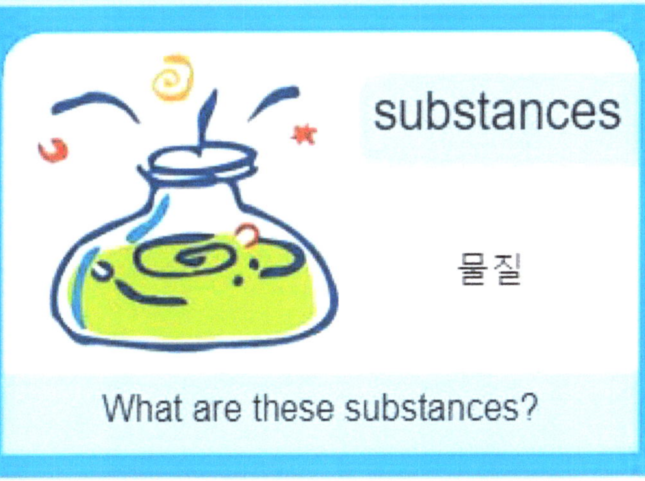

substances

물질

What are these substances?

suffix

접미사

What is the suffix of the word?

sugar

설탕

Sugar cube for your tea?

tools

도구

May I borrow your tools?

total

합계

What's the total?

track

과정

The runners got on the track.

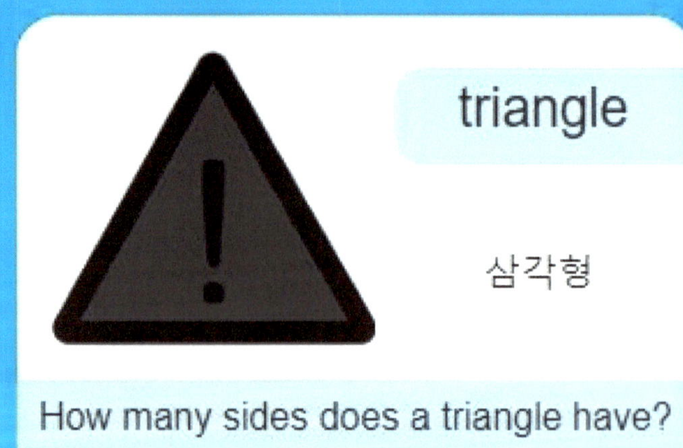

triangle

삼각형

How many sides does a triangle have?

truck

트럭

Is thaty our truck?

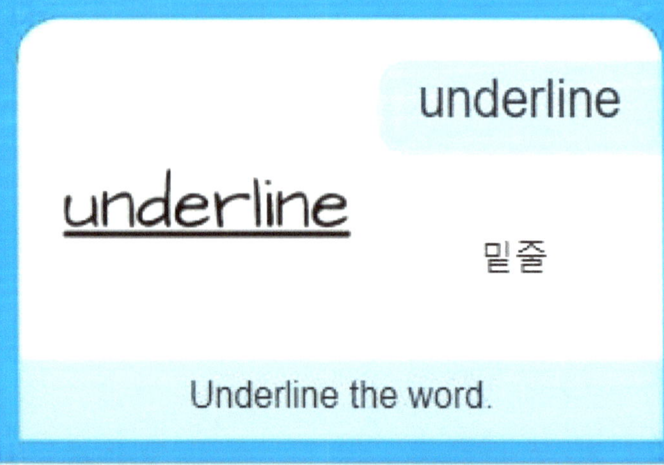

underline

<u>underline</u>

밑줄

Underline the word.

various

여러

I watch various shows.

view

전망

That is a beautiful view!

Washington

워싱턴

She is from Washington.

we'll

의지

We'll finish buying our groceries.

western

서부 사람

It's western wear day.

win

승리

Did you win?

woman

여자

The woman was on her way to work.

workers

노동자

The workers were busy.

wouldn't

아니

Wouldn't you like to go shopping?

wrong

잘못된

Did I get it wrong?

yellow

노랑

A banana is yellow.

after

후

You may have dessert after dinner.

again

다시

May we go on the ride again?

air

공기

The air was cold.

also

또한

I also like baseball.

America

미국

Columbus sailed to America.

animal

동물

My favorite animal is a lion.

another

다른

Have another cookie.

answer

대답

Raise your hand to answer.

any

어떤

Do you have any crayons?

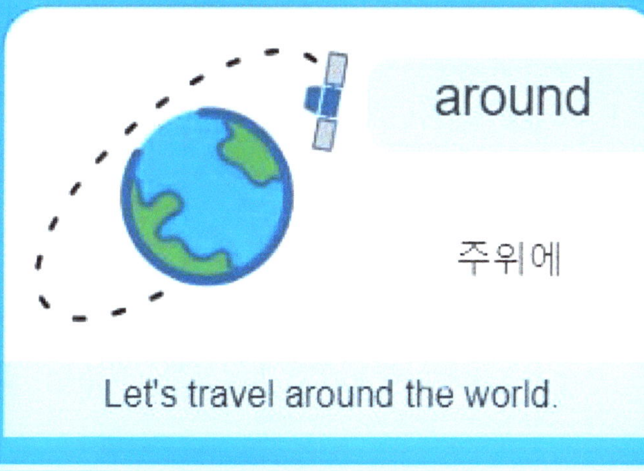

around

주위에

Let's travel around the world.

ask

물어보기

It's good to ask questions.

away

떨어져

Throw your trash away.

back

뒤

We went back to school.

because

때문에

I went to bed because I was tired.

before

전에

Sharpen your pencil before the test.

big

큰

The elephant is a big animal.

boy

소년

The boy played a basketball.

came

왔다

He came to class.

change

변화

I save my change.

different

다른

They use different balls.

does

하다

Does he ride the bus?

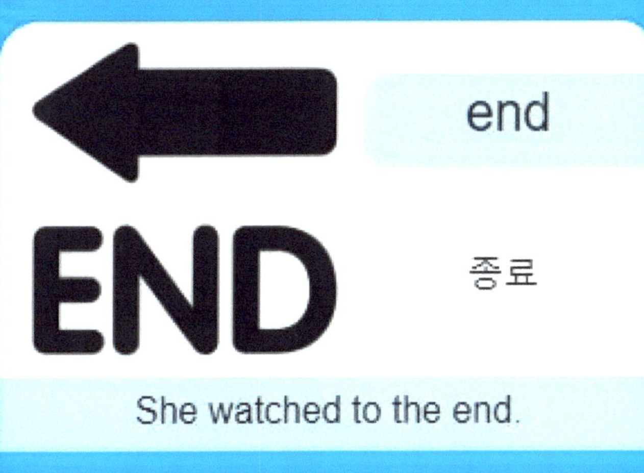

end
종료

She watched to the end.

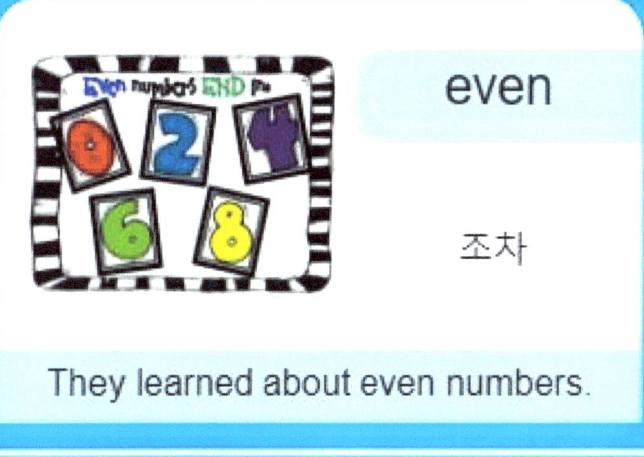

even
조차

They learned about even numbers.

follow
따르다

Follow the teacher.

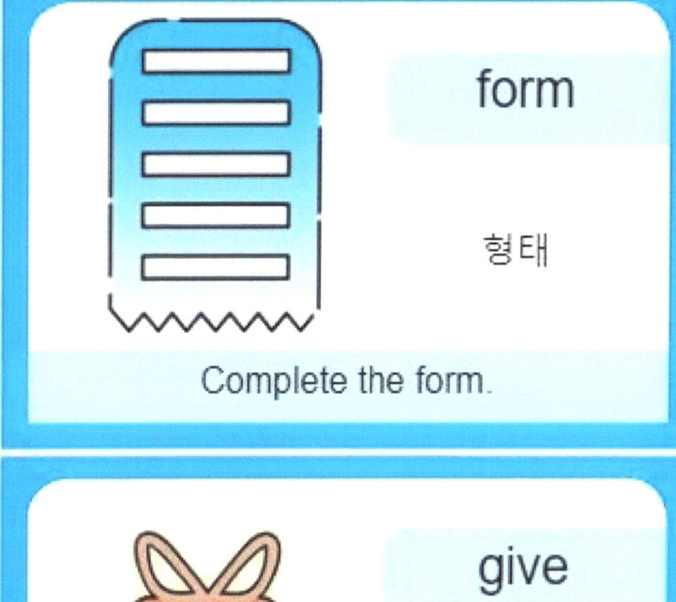

form
형태

Complete the form.

found
녹이다

We found a puppy.

give
주기

I like to give gifts.

good
좋은

The hamburger was good.

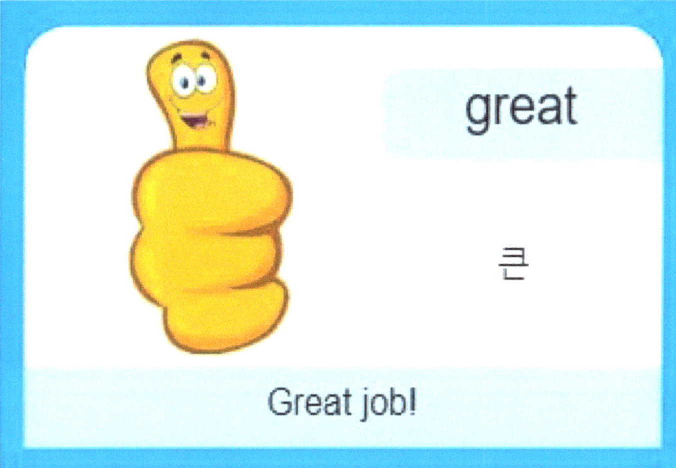

great
큰

Great job!

hand
손
Please hand in your work.

help
도움
You should help others.

here
여기
Do you sit here?

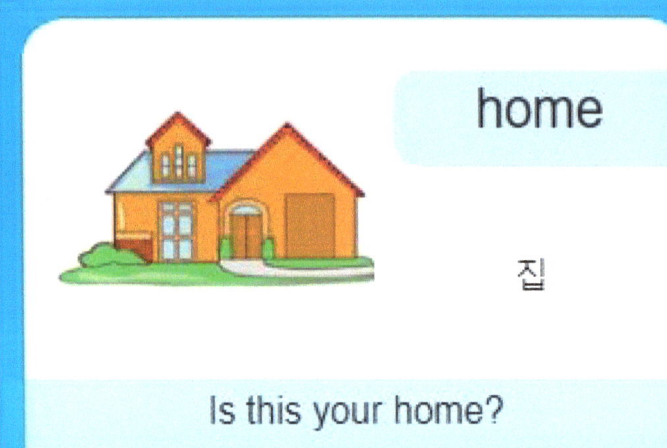

home
집
Is this your home?

house
집
The doll house was pink.

just
다만
The train just left.

kind
친절하게 대해
Be kind to each other.

know
알고있다
I don't know.

land

땅

They bought some land.

large

큰

A bear is large.

learn

배우다

It's fun to learn science.

letter

편지

He mailed a letter.

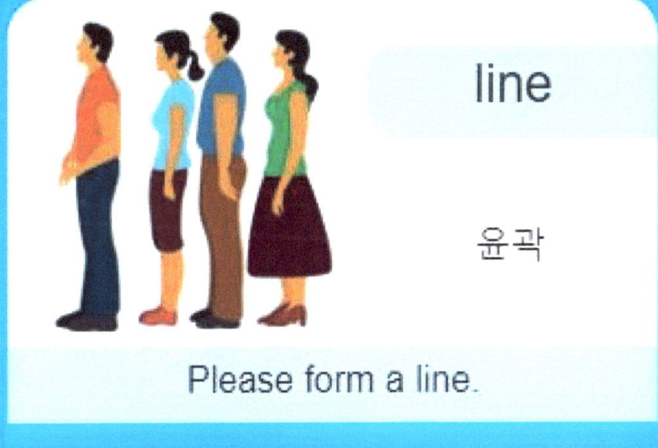

line

윤곽

Please form a line.

little

작은

He has a little sister.

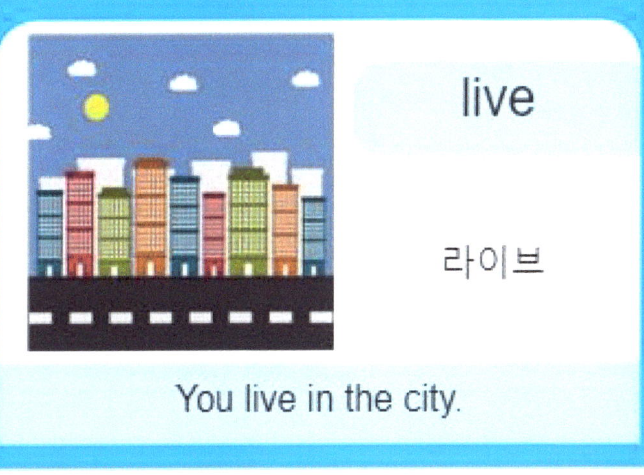

live

라이브

You live in the city.

man

남자

The man drove.

me

나를

Come with me to the park.

means

방법

She got her by means of a taxi.

men

남자들

The men played football.

most

대부분

Most students like to help.

mother

어머니

He loves his mother.

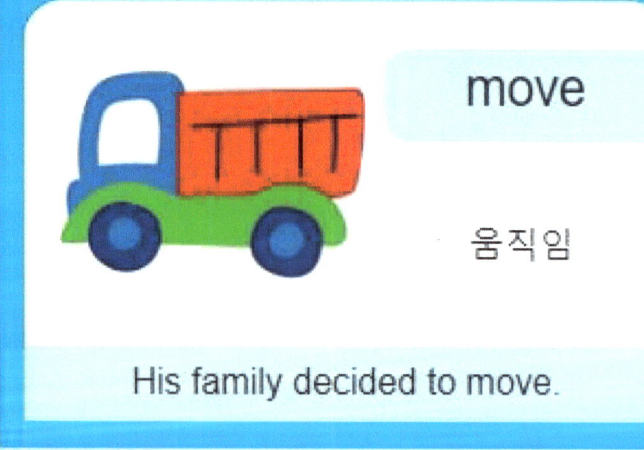

move

움직임

His family decided to move.

much

많은

How much is the camera?

must

해야한다

You must raise your hand.

name

이름

What is his name?

need

필요

Do you need to sleep?

new

새로운

We have a new teacher.

off

떨어져서

The rocket blasted off.

old

낡은

Those are old toys.

only

뿐

There's only one slice left.

our

우리의

She was our teacher.

over

위에

He jumped over it.

page

페이지

Please turn the page.

picture

그림

They took their picture.

place

장소

This is my favorite place.

play

플레이

Let's play together!

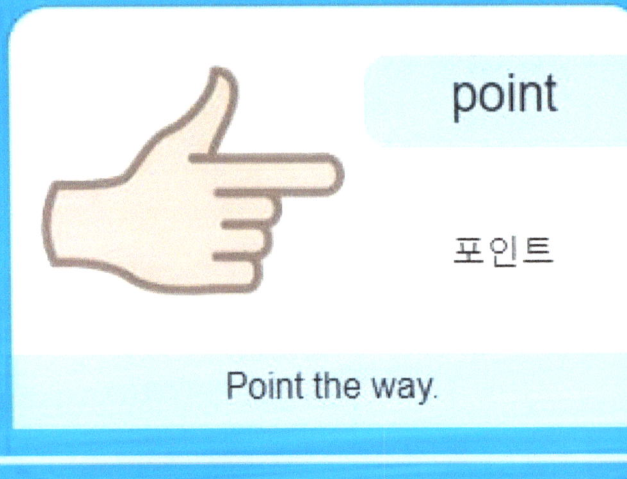

point

포인트

Point the way.

put

놓다

Please put the supplies away.

read

읽다

Do you like to read?

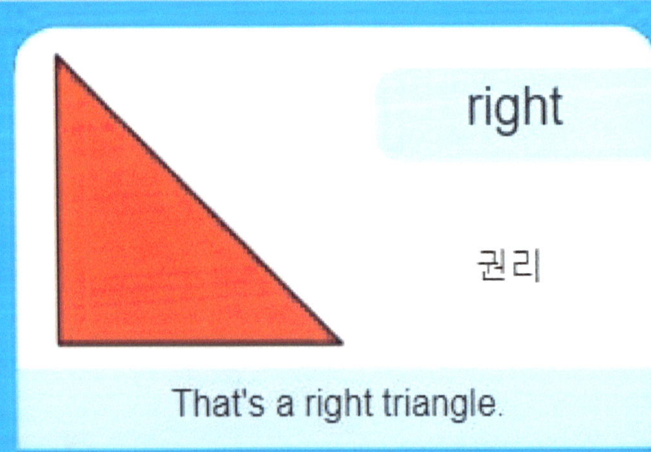

right

권리

That's a right triangle.

same

같은

Did you get the same answer?

say

말하다

What did you say?

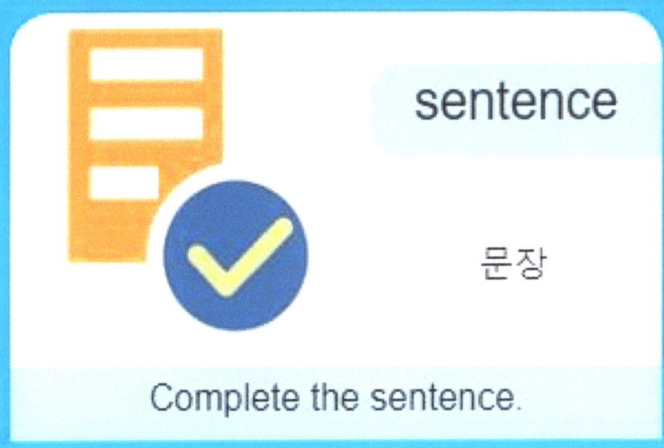

sentence

문장

Complete the sentence.

set

세트

Please set the table.

should

할까요

We should exercise.

show

보여 주다

Show your work.

small

작은

The ladybug is small.

sound

소리

A bee makes a buzzing sound.

spell

주문

Please spell the word.

still

아직도

I still want ice skates.

study

연구

It's time to study.

such

이러한

He is such a good dog.

take

갖다

Please take your seat.

tell

텔

She wanted to tell a secret.

things

소지품

She washed a lot of things.

think

생각한다

Think about it.

three

세

It's the number three.

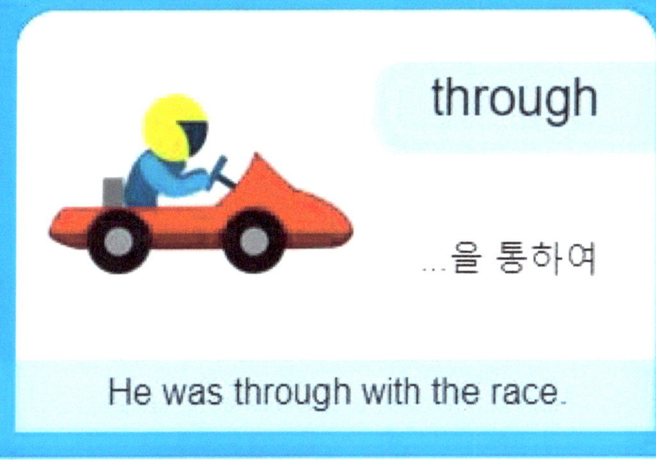

through

...을 통하여

He was through with the race.

too

너무

Do you like chocolate too?

try

시험

Try again, please.

turn

회전

Turn in your homework.

us

우리

She taught us.

very

대단히

He is a very good singer.

want

필요

I want to ride my bike.

well

잘

You did well.

went

갔다

We went to recess.

where

어디

Where do you want to go?

why

왜

She asked why?

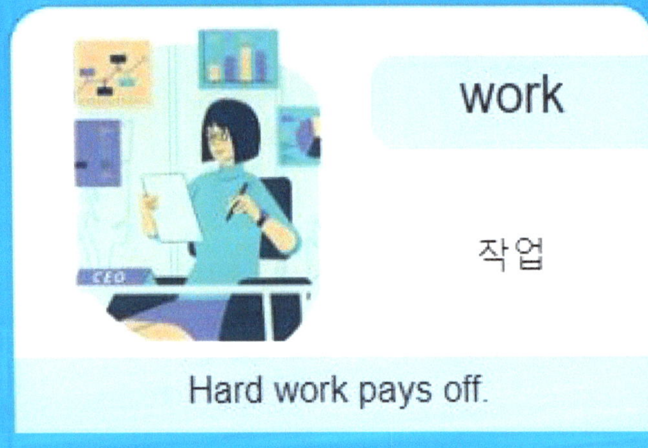

work

작업

Hard work pays off.

world

세계

I want to travel the world.

years

연령

You are five years old today.

above

이상

The sky was above them.

add

더하다

If you add one plus two, you get three.

almost

거의

It's almost lunch time.

along

...을 따라서

We get along.

always

항상

She always brushes her teeth.

began

시작했다

The baby began to cry.

begin

시작하다

You may begin your exam.

being

존재

She is being shy.

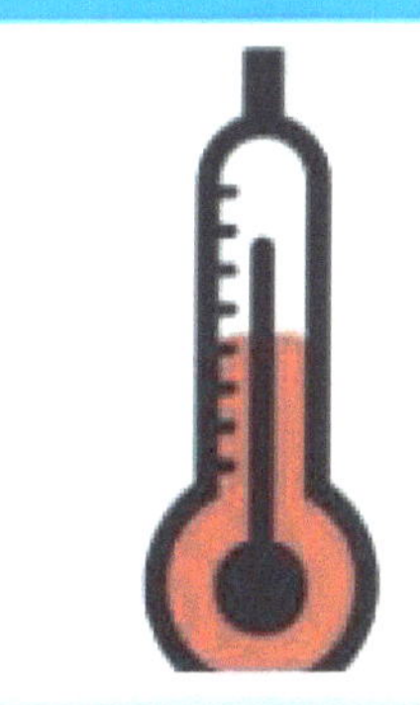

below

이하

It's below thirty degrees.

between

중에서

Two is between one and three.

book

책

I'm reading this book.

both

양자 모두

They both worked on math.

car

차

He bought a new car.

carry

나르다

She had a bag to carry her groceries.

children

어린이

Four children sang.

city

시티

He worked in the city.

close

닫기

Please close the door.

country

국가

Do you live in the country?

cut

절단

You use scissors to cut.

don't

아니

Don't forget!

earth

지구

Our planet is Earth.

eat

먹다

I eat bananas.

enough

충분히

Did you eat enough pancakes?

every

...마다

I shower every day.

example

예

This is an example of a bird.

eyes

눈

What color are her eyes?

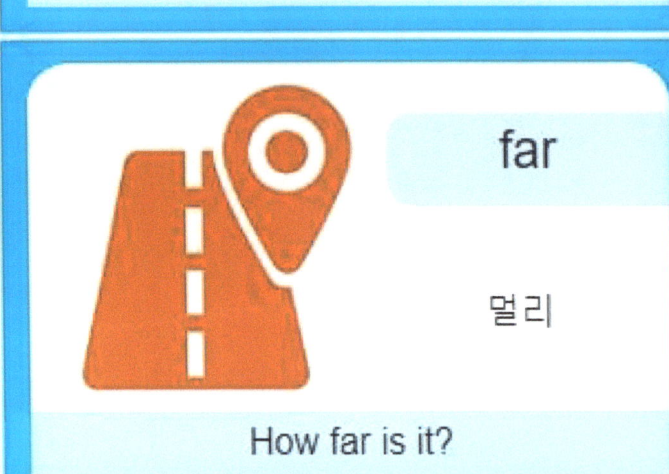

face

얼굴

They were at the face painting booth.

family

가족

How big is your family?

far

멀리

How far is it?

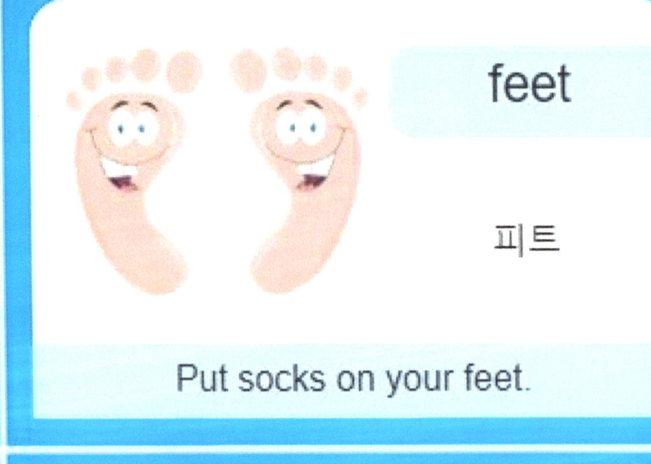

father

아버지

Her father walked her to school.

feet

피트

Put socks on your feet.

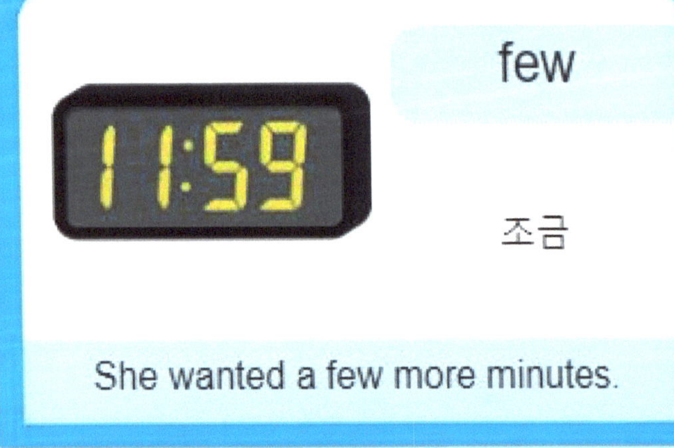

few

조금

She wanted a few more minutes.

food

음식

They made a lot of food.

There were four of them.

The girl wore pink shoes.

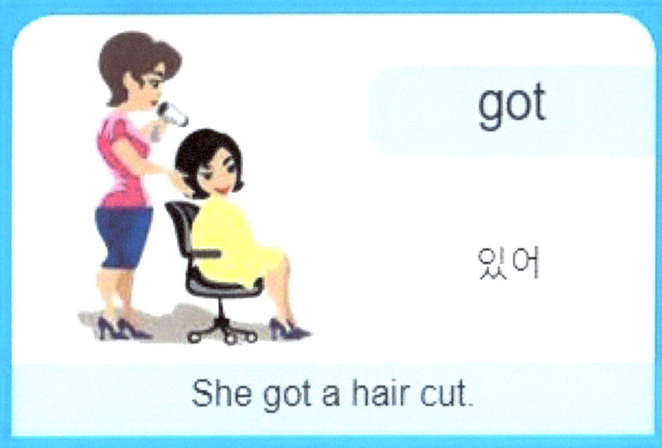

She got a hair cut.

They were working in a group.

The plant began to grow.

He wore a hard hat.

He wore a cap on his head.

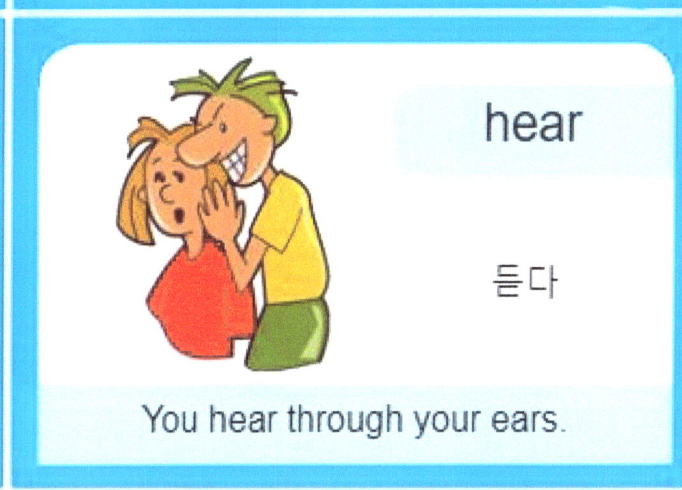

You hear through your ears.

high
높은
She wore high heels.

idea
생각
I have an idea!

important
중대한
It's important!

Indian
인도 사람
It's an Indian elephant.

it's
이다
It's a tiger cub.

keep
유지
Can you keep a secret?

last
마지막
It's the last day of school.

late
늦은
You're late.

leave

떠나다

He packed to leave.

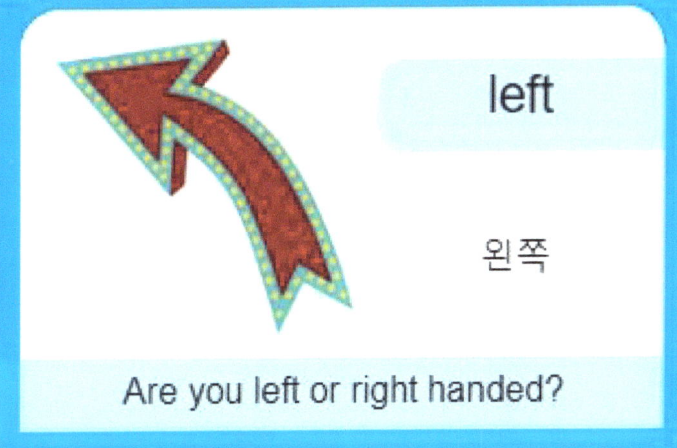

left

왼쪽

Are you left or right handed?

let

허락하다

Will you let me go fishing?

life

생명

Life is about friends and family.

light

빛

The light turned yellow.

list

명부

Here's my to-do list

might

힘

It might rain today.

mile

마일

It's a mile from here.

miss

미스...

You may correct any you miss.

mountains

산

There are alot of mountains here.

near

근처에

We are near the beach.

never

못

I've never broken my leg.

next

다음

Take the next step.

night

밤

You can see the stars at night.

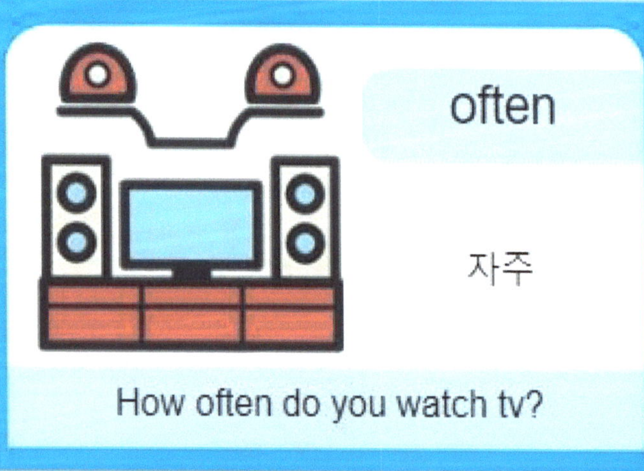

often

자주

How often do you watch tv?

once

한번

Once upon a time...

open

열다

The door is open.

own

개인적인

Do you own a computer?

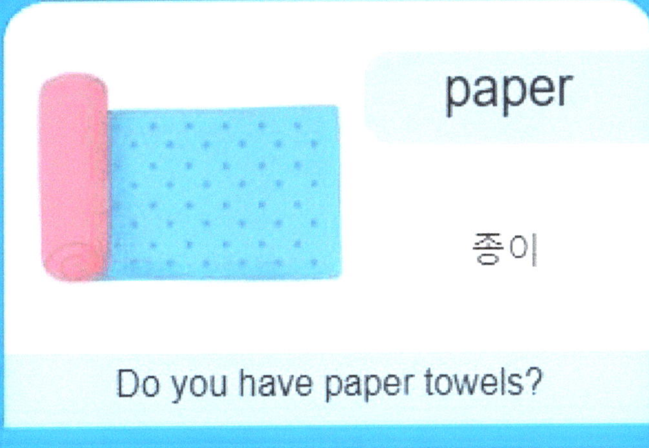

paper

종이

Do you have paper towels?

plant

식물

I will water the plant.

real

레알

Her real name is Sally.

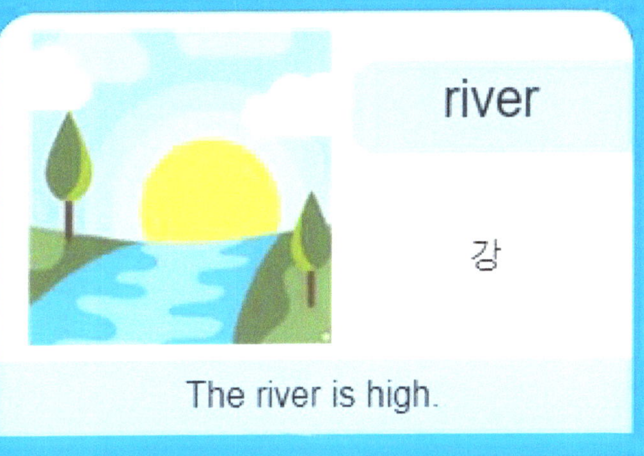

river

강

The river is high.

run

운영

He likes to run with his dog.

saw

보다

We saw a UFO.

school

학교

Do you like school?

sea

바다

The ship is at sea.

second

둘째

She won second place.

seem

보다

You seem busy.

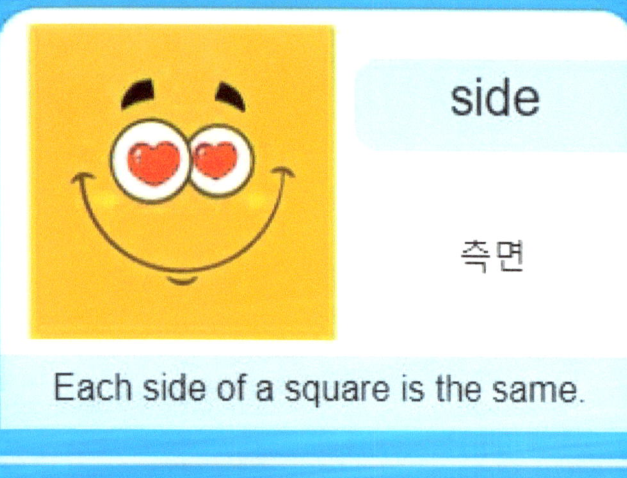

side

측면

Each side of a square is the same.

something

어떤 것

Did you hear something?

sometimes

때때로

Sometimes we watch tv.

song

노래

We will sing a song.

soon

곧

Dinner will be ready soon.

start

스타트

Start writing.

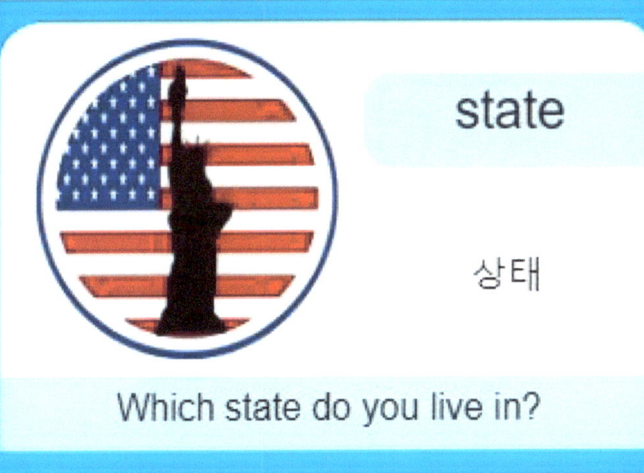

state

상태

Which state do you live in?

stop

중지

Do you see the stop sign?

story

이야기

What's the story about?

talk

이야기

Let's talk.

those

그

Those are great cookies!

thought

생각

I thought the novel was good.

together

함께

They went shopping together.

took

갖다

He took the last piece.

tree

나무

Did you decorate the tree?

under

아래에

It lives under the sea.

until

...까지

I work until 5 o'clock.

walk

산책

We went for a walk.

watch

손목 시계

Do you wear a watch?

while

동안

We had fun while skiing.

white

하얀

They drew on the white board.

without

없이

I can't go without my backpack.

young

젊은

Her kids are young.

across

건너서

It's across the street.

against

에 맞서

It's against the rules.

area

지역

There are no wild animals in this area.

become

지다

It will become a butterfly.

best

베스트

Do your best!

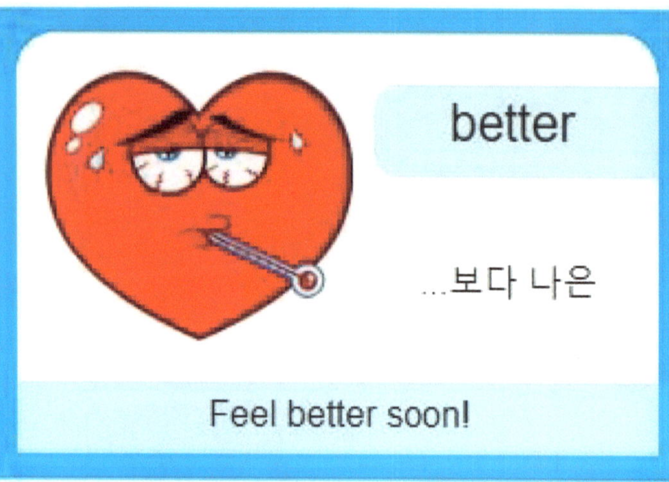

better
...보다 나은
Feel better soon!

birds
새
There's a lot of birds.

black
검은
He has a black cat.

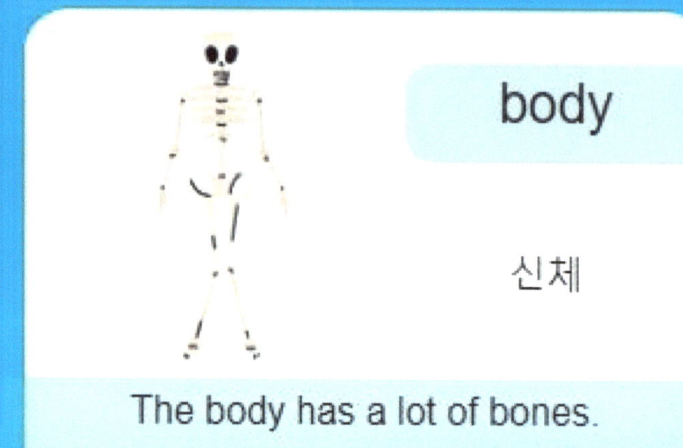

body
신체
The body has a lot of bones.

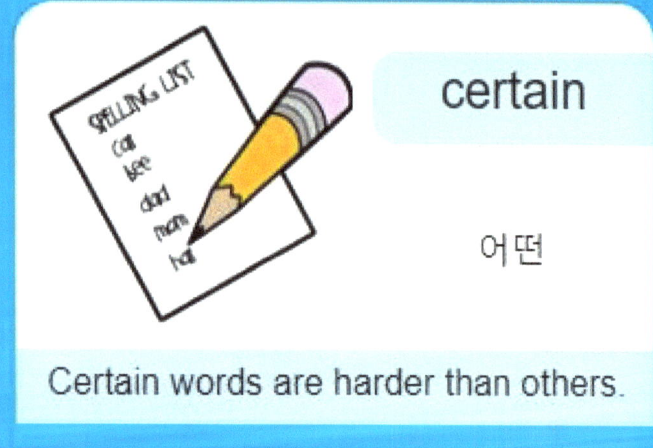

certain
어떤
Certain words are harder than others.

cold
춥다
It's cold outside.

color
색깔
What is your favorite color?

complete
완전한
Did you complete your workout?

www.ingramcontent.com/pod-product-compliance
Lightning Source LLC
Chambersburg PA
CBHW042007110726
48006CB00004B/1002